The Life and Work of
Paul Klee

Sean Connolly

Heinemann Library
Chicago, Illinois

Customer Service 888-454-2279
Visit our website at www.heinemannraintree.com

Designed by Jo Malivoire and Q2A Creative
Printed in China by South China Printing Company

10 09 08 07 06
10 9 8 7 6 5 4 3 2 1

New edition ISBN: 1-40348-496-1 (hardcover)
                      1-40348-507-0 (paperback)

The Library of Congress has cataloged the first edition as follows:
Connolly, Sean, 1956-
        Paul Klee / Sean Connolly.
                p. cm. — (The life and work of–) (Heinemann profiles)
        Includes bibliographical references and index.
        Summary: Introduces the life and work of Paul Klee, discussing his early years, life in Switzerland and Germany, and development as an artist.
        ISBN 1-57572-952-0 (Lib. binding)
        1. Klee, Paul, 1879-1940 Juvenile literature. 2. Artists-Germany Biography
Juvenile literature. [1. Klee, Paul, 1879-1940. 2. Artists
3. Painting, German. 4. Art appreciation]
I. Title. II. Series. III. Series: Heinemann profiles.
N6888.K55C665   1999
760'. 092—dc21   99-14548
[B]   CIP

Acknowledgments
The author and publishers are grateful to the following for permission to reproduce copyright material:
AKG Photo, pp. 4, 10, 22, 24 Paul-Klee-Stiftung, Kunstmuseum, Bern/L Moillet, p. 20. Fotopress/Walter Henggeler, p. 28; Page 5, Paul Klee *Familienspaziergang, 1930, 264*, Credit: Paul-Klee-Stiftung, Kunstmuseum, Bern. Page 7, Paul Klee *Dünen landschaft, 1921, 139*, Credit: Paul-Klee-Stiftung, Kunstmuseum, Bern. Page 9, Paul Klee *Schadau, 1895/96*, Credit: Paul-Klee-Stiftung, Kunstmuseum, Bern. Page 11, Paul Klee *Siebzehn, irr. 1923*, Credit: Oeffentliche Kunstsammlung Kupferstichkabinett, Basel. Page 13, Paul Klee *Meine Bude, 1896*, Credit: Paul-Klee-Stiftung, Kunstmuseum, Bern. Page 15, Paul Klee *Lily, 1905, 32*, Credit: Paul-Klee-Stiftung, Kunstmuseum, Bern. Page 17, Paul Klee, *Candide 7. Capitel "Il lève le voile d'une main timide" 1911, 63*, Credit: Paul-Klee-Stiftung, Kunstmuseum, Bern. Page 19, Paul Klee *Mädchen mit Krügen*, Credit: Paul-Klee-Stiftung, Kunstmuseum, Bern. Page 21, Paul Klee *Rote und Weisse Kuppeln, 1914, 45*, Credit: AKG Photo. Page 23, Paul Klee *Einst dem Grau der Nacht enttaucht…, 1918, 17*, Credit: Paul-Klee-Stiftung, Kunstmuseum, Bern. Page 25, Paul Klee *Plan einer garten-architektur, 1920, 214*, Credit: Bridgeman Art Library. Page 27, Paul Klee *Polyphon gefasstes Weiss, 1930, 140(x10)*, Credit: Paul-Klee-Stiftung, Kunstmuseum, Bern. Page 29, Paul Klee *TOD und FEUER, 1940, 332 (G 12)*, Credit: Paul-Klee-Stiftung, Kunstmuseum, Bern.

Cover: *Large Chessboard* by Paul Klee, reproduced with permission of Rahmenleisten Kunsthaus Zürich.

The publishers would like to thank Nancy Harris for her assistance in the preparation of this book.

Every effort has been made to contact copyright holders of any material reproduced in this book. Any omissions will be rectified in subsequent printings if notice is given to the publisher.

The paper used to print this book comes from sustainable sources.

Some words in this book are in bold, **like this.** You can find out what they mean by looking in the Glossary.

Contents

Who was Paul Klee?

Paul Klee was a
Swiss painter and
graphic artist.
He liked to make
very colorful
paintings. His
pictures make
people think
of music
and dreams.

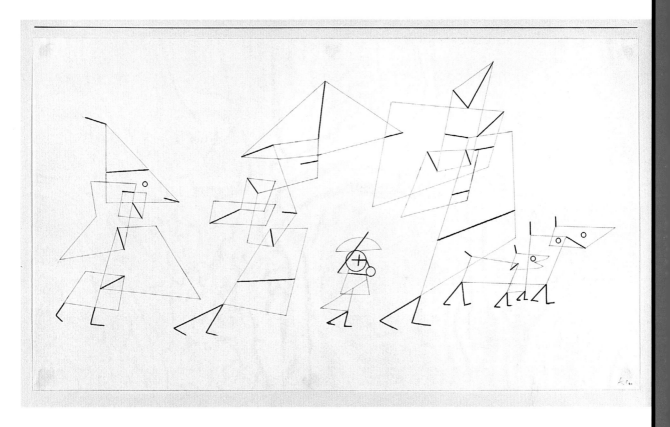

Paul kept a sense of fun in his paintings.
This picture shows how he liked to "take
a line for a walk."

Early Years

Paul Klee was born on December 18 1879 near the city of Berne in Switzerland. His family loved music. Paul learned to play the violin when he was seven years old.

1923 139 Dünen landschaft

Paul's uncle Ernst had a café. Paul liked
to look at the patterns on the tablecloths
there. He made this painting in 1923. It
shows Paul was still interested in patterns.

School Days

Paul went to school in Berne. He still enjoyed music. He joined the Berne **Orchestra** when he was only 10 years old.

Paul also began to enjoy drawing pictures. He filled his school notebooks with drawings and designs. He tried to show his love of music and poetry in his paintings.

The Move to Germany

Paul left school when he was 19. He moved to Munich in Germany. There he began to **study** drawing and painting. Magazines like this one helped him to think of funny ideas.

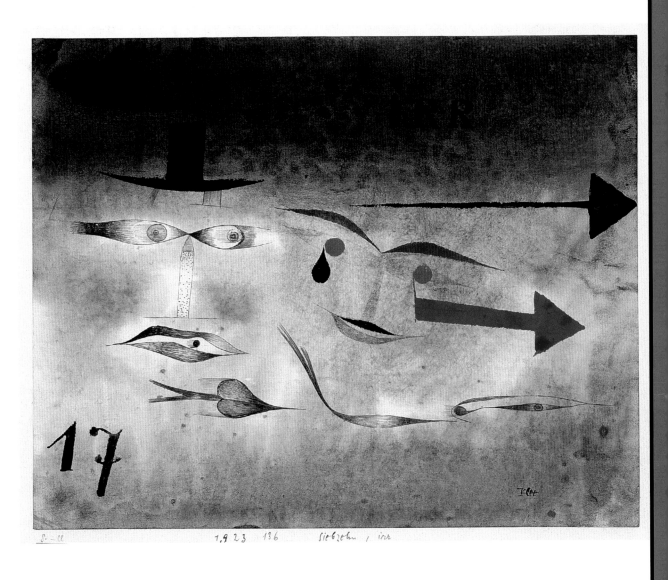

Paul had a good sense of fun. He made
this picture in 1923. He was 44 years old.
It shows some interesting faces.

Learning to Paint

In 1901 Paul **studied** paintings in Italy. He then returned to his family in Berne. There he **practiced** his own art and tried out many different ideas.

Most of Paul's works were drawings or **etchings**. This drawing of his bedroom shows how well Paul could draw.

A Growing Family

In 1906 Paul married Lily Stumpf. Their son Felix was born a year later. Lily earned money by playing piano **concerts**. Paul worked at home.

This is a painting of Lily. Paul **exhibited** some of his pictures in 1906. He became better known after the exhibition.

Public Success

Paul's first one-man **exhibition** was in Berne in 1910. It was a great success. The same exhibition was then shown in other Swiss cities.

Paul's pictures were black and white. He used an ink pen and drew on white paper. This picture was used in a book.

A Friendly Welcome

Paul became friends with two other artists, August Macke and Wassily Kandinsky. Paul joined their group of **expressionist** artists. The group was called *Der Blaue Reiter* (*The Blue Rider*).

Paul also liked the work of other artists. He painted this picture in 1910. It looks like a painting by an artist called Paul Cézanne.

Color Takes Hold

In 1914 Paul and August Macke visited Tunisia in Africa. Paul loved the bright light and colors there. He decided to stop using just black and white in his pictures.

The colored squares in this painting look like the **mosaics** Paul saw in Tunisia. Mosaics are pictures made out of squares of colored stone.

New Directions

Paul was happy painting in many colors. He felt free to try some other new ideas. He started putting letters and numbers in his pictures.

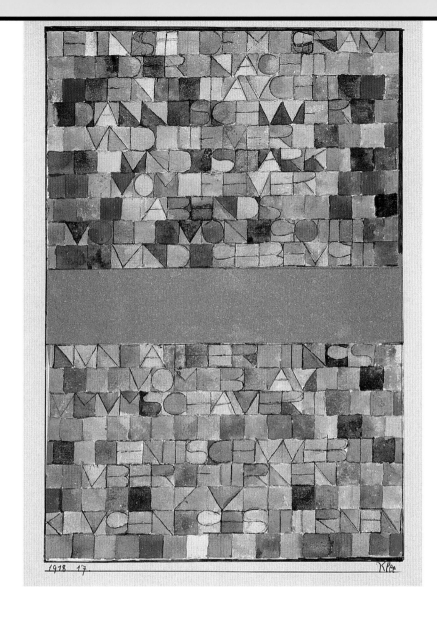

Paul thought numbers and letters made people think of words and dreams. Paul felt he was making a new **language** in his pictures.

Time as a Teacher

In 1920 Paul became a teacher at the
Bauhaus. This was the most famous art
school in Germany. Paul taught there
until 1931.

Paul's pictures show what he taught at the Bauhaus. He taught students that an artist is like a tree trunk. The branches are the thoughts he shows in his pictures.

Escape from Germany

A new **government**, called the **Nazis**, took power in Germany. They did not like Paul's pictures or those of many other artists. In 1933 Paul had to move to Switzerland.

The Nazis wanted pictures to look like real things. Paul did not agree. He used his colors and lines to make people think for themselves.

Illness and Death

Paul caught a disease when he was 56 years old. He never got better. He still painted, but he was always in pain. Paul died on June 29 1940. He was 61 years old.

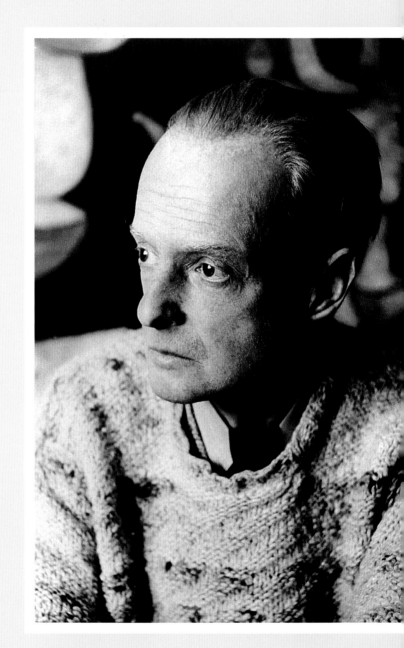

Paul's illness made him think about death. His pictures became darker. Thick black lines replaced the bright colors he used when he was well.

Timeline

1879	Paul Klee is born near Berne, Switzerland on December 18.
1886	Paul begins to **study** the violin.
1889	Paul joins Berne Municipal **Orchestra**.
1898	Paul leaves school and moves to Munich, Germany.
1906	Paul marries Lily Stumpf and has **etchings exhibited**.
1910	Paul has successful exhibitions in Switzerland.
1911	Paul joins *Der Blaue Reiter* group of **expressionist** artists.
1914	Paul visits Tunisia and decides to fill his pictures with color.
1914–18	World War I.
1920–31	Paul teaches at the famous Bauhaus art school in Germany.
1933	Paul is forced to leave Germany and go to Switzerland.
1935	Paul becomes sick.
1939	World War II begins in Europe.
1940	Paul dies in Muralto, Switzerland on June 29.

Glossary

concert playing music in public

etching picture made by drawing on a metal plate and then printing it

exhibit to show and sell works of art in public

exhibition public showing of paintings

expressionist type of art that changes the way things look to show feelings

government group of people who rule a country

graphic artist someone who makes pictures to print

language way of passing on ideas to other people

mosaic pattern of colored stones used to make a picture

Nazi short name for the National Socialist German Workers' Party

orchestra group of musicians who play concerts in public

practice keep trying to do something to get better at it

study learn about a subject

More Books to Read

Wolfe, Gillian. *Oxford First Book of Art.* New York: OUP, 2004.

Conolly, Sean. *The Life and Work of Paul Cézanne.* Chicago: Heinemann Library, 2006.

More Paintings to See

New House in the Suburbs, 1924. National Gallery of Art, Washington, D.C.

Land of Lemons, 1929. The Philips Collection, Washington, D.C.

Trees Behind Rocks, 1929. The Solomon R. Gugggenheim Museum, New York City, N.Y.

Index